Contents

Living with uncertainty
Unit guide

The School Mathematics Project

The right of the
University of Cambridge
to print and sell
all manner of books
was granted by
Henry VIII in 1534.
The University has printed
and published continuously
since 1584.

Cambridge University Press

Cambridge New York Port Chester Melbourne Sydney

Main authors	Chris Belsom	With contributions from
	Stan Dolan	
	Chris Little	Robert Black
	Mary Rouncefield	David Cundy
		Jackie Gallard
		Howard Gilbert
		Sarah Lightfoot
		Fiona McGill
		Paul Roder

Team Leader	Chris Belsom
Project Director	Stan Dolan
Statistics programs	Margaret and Peter Hayball

The authors would like to give special thanks to Ann White for her help in producing the trial edition and in preparing this book for publication.

Published by the Press Syndicate of the University of Cambridge
The Pitt Building, Trumpington Street, Cambridge CB2 1RP
40 West 20th Street, New York, NY10011–4211, USA
10 Stamford Road, Oakleigh, Melbourne 3166, Australia

© Cambridge University Press 1991

First published 1991

Produced by Gecko Limited, Bicester, Oxon.

Cover design by Iguana Creative Design

Printed in Great Britain at the University Press, Cambridge

British Library cataloguing in publication data

16–19 mathematics.
Living with uncertainty. Unit guide
1. Statistical mathematics
I. School Mathematics Project
519.5

ISBN 0 521 40876 8

Introduction to 16–19 Mathematics

Nobody reads introductions and nobody reads teachers' guides, so what chance does the introduction to this Unit Guide have? The least we can do is to keep it short! We hope that you will find the discussion point and tasksheet commentaries and ideas on presentation and enrichment useful.

The School Mathematics Project was founded in 1961 with the purpose of improving the teaching of mathematics in schools by the provision of new course materials. SMP authors are experienced teachers and each new venture is tested by schools in a draft version before publication. Work on *16–19 Mathematics* started in 1986 and the pilot of the course has been used by over 30 schools since 1987.

Since its inception the SMP has always offered an 'after sales service' for teachers using its materials. If you have any comments on *16–19 Mathematics*, or would like advice on its use, please write to:

16–19 Mathematics
The SMP Office
The University
Southampton SO9 5NH

Why 16–19 Mathematics?

A major problem in mathematics education is how to enable ordinary mortals to comprehend in a few years concepts which geniuses have taken centuries to develop. In theory, our view of how to pass on this body of knowledge effectively and pleasurably has changed considerably; but no great revolution in practice has been seen in sixth-form classrooms generally. We hope that in this course, the change in approach to mathematics teaching embodied in GCSE schemes will be carried forward. The principles applied in the course are appropriate to this aim.

- Students are actively involved in developing mathematical ideas.
- Premature abstraction and over-reliance on algorithms are avoided.
- Wherever possible, problems arise from, or at least relate to, everyday life.
- Appropriate use is made of modern technology such as graphic calculators and microcomputers.
- Misunderstandings are confronted and acted upon.
  By applying these principles and presenting material in an attractive way, A level mathematics is made more accessible to students and more meaningful to them as individuals. The *16–19 Mathematics* course is flexible enough to provide for the whole range of students who obtain at least a grade C at GCSE.

Structure of the courses

The A and AS level courses have a core-plus-options structure.
Details of the full range of possibilities, including A and AS level
Further Mathematics courses, may be obtained from the Joint
Matriculation Board, Manchester M15 6EU.

For the A level course *Mathematics (Pure with Applications)*, students
must study eight core units and a further two optional units. The
structure diagram below shows how the units are related to each
other. Other optional units are being developed to give students an
opportunity to study aspects of mathematics which are appropriate
to their personal interests and enthusiasms.

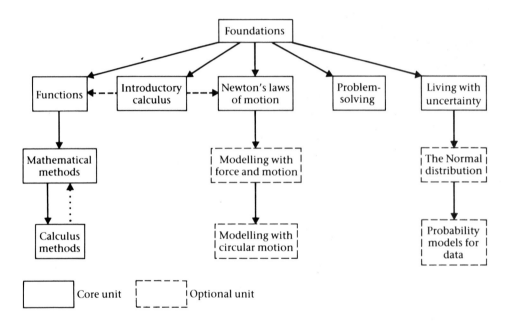

The *Foundations* unit should be started before or at the same time as
any other core unit.

Any of the other units can be started at the same time as the
Foundations unit. The second half of *Functions* requires prior
coverage of *Introductory calculus*. *Newton's laws of motion* requires
calculus notation which is covered in the initial chapters of
Introductory calculus.

The Polynomial approximations chapter in *Mathematical methods*
requires prior coverage of some sections of *Calculus methods*.

For the AS level *Mathematics (Pure with Applications)* course, students
must study *Foundations*, *Introductory calculus* and *Functions*. Students
must then study a further two applied units.

Material

In traditional mathematics texts the theory has been written in a didactic manner for passive reading, in the hope that it will be accepted and understood – or, more realistically, that the teacher will supply the necessary motivation and deal with problems of understanding. In marked contrast, *16–19 Mathematics* adopts a questing mode, demanding the active participation of students. The textbooks contain several new devices to aid a more active style of learning.

• Topics are opened up through **group discussion points**, signalled in the text by the symbol

and enclosed in rectangular frames. These consist of pertinent questions to be discussed by students, with guidance and help from the teacher. Commentaries for discussion points are included in this unit guide.

• The text is also punctuated by **thinking points**, having the shape

and again containing questions. These should be dealt with by students without the aid of the teacher. In facing up to the challenge offered by the thinking points it is intended that students will achieve a deeper insight and understanding. A solution within the text confirms or modifies the student's response to each thinking point.

• At appropriate points in the text, students are referred to **tasksheets** which are placed at the end of the relevant chapter. A tasksheet usually consists of a self-contained piece of work which is used to investigate a concept prior to any formal exposition. In many cases, it takes up an idea raised in a discussion point, examining it in more detail and preparing the way for formal treatment. There are also **extension tasksheets** (labelled by an E), for higher attaining students, which investigate a topic in more depth and **supplementary tasksheets** (labelled by an S), which are intended to help students with a relatively weak background in a particular topic. Commentaries for all the tasksheets are included in this unit guide.

The aim of the **exercises** is to check full understanding of principles and give the student confidence through reinforcement of his or her understanding.

Graphic calculators/microcomputers are used throughout the course. In particular, much use is made of graph plotters. The use of videos and equipment for practical work is also recommended.

As well as the textbooks and unit guides, there is a *Teacher's resource file*. This file contains:

- review sheets which may be used for homework or tests;

- datasheets;

- technology datasheets which give help with using particular calculators or pieces of software;

- a programme of worksheets for more able students which would, in particular, help prepare them for the STEP examination.

Introduction to the unit (for the teacher)

This unit has been written as an introduction to the ideas of statistics and probability. It provides a complete course for those students who will study no further statistics, but is also the foundation on which other statistics units of the *16–19 Mathematics* course build.

Although some elementary mathematical results are developed, the unit should be easily accessible to a student with a background of GCSE mathematics and some of the ideas in the early chapters may already have been encountered in the GCSE course. This material will provide a reassuring start but should not be laboured for the more able student.

There is ample opportunity for computer simulations and for practical work (for example, experiments where data is collected). It would be advantageous, though not essential, to have a computer available in the classroom and it may be appropriate for the teacher to encourage the use of a suitable computer package for some of the work on data analysis. The use of calculators is encouraged throughout: indeed, this has influenced the development of the teaching material. Although sufficient data sources are provided, students should be encouraged to provide their own data, perhaps from their work in other subjects.

Chapter 1

The aim of the introductory chapter is to give some indication of the importance of statistics in daily life and to point out the central role of probabilistic ideas in modern scientific thought.

In one of the tasksheets, it is suggested that students should write a short newspaper article based on given data. This may, of course, be replaced by anything more topical, perhaps with an actual article for comparison.

Chapter 2

Data analysis is introduced and students are encouraged to make a quick visual impression of data before conducting a more detailed analysis. Stem and leaf diagrams and box plots are introduced, together with numerical representation of data through the mean, median and mode. Interesting mathematical properties of the mean and median, which are relevant to work done in other parts of the course, are considered.

Chapter 3

In this chapter, data analysis is studied in greater depth. The use of histograms as a means of representing distributions is discussed and the concept of frequency density developed. Measures of spread are considered, with a stress on considering **what** these are measuring. Sigma notation is introduced and both forms of the variance formula are developed. It is emphasised that standard deviation is the most important and useful measure of spread.

Chapter 4

Elementary ideas in probability are studied to consolidate an understanding of the underlying concepts. The ideas of a random variable and its probability distribution are introduced and the mean and variance of the random variable are defined.

Experiments with *Chance cards* are followed by computer simulations of the card experiments. The distinction between continuous and discrete variables is made, with the remainder of the unit focusing on discrete variables only.

Chapter 5

This chapter is concerned with combining probabilities for compound events. The important concept of independence is introduced and the addition and multiplication laws are developed. The chapter ends with the binomial probability model. The modelling aspect is stressed and there is an emphasis on the assumptions that are necessary before the model can be applied.

Chapter 6

This chapter considers some of the problems of sampling and should lead, for example, to a more critical appraisal of the results of opinion polls and surveys. There is a brief introduction to the concept of statistical significance. The need for random samples is demonstrated through a number of short practical activities. In situations where the binomial model is appropriate, the significance of the results is assessed by considering the results of simulations of the surveys.

Tasksheets and resources

This list gives an overview of where tasksheets are to be used. Items in *italics* refer to resources not included in the main text.

- The statistics software may be ordered from Cambridge University Press.

- The Chance cards are three packs of cards, each containing 40 numbered cards. The distributions are as follows.

Yellow					Red					Blue				
Number	1	2	3	4	Number	1	2	3	4	Number	1	2	3	4
No. in pack	16	12	8	4	No. in pack	10	10	10	10	No. in pack	10	20	10	–

Such packs can easily be made up using blank cards from an educational supplier. To colour-code the packs, use different coloured pens when writing the numbers on the cards.

- The other italicised items can be found in the *Teacher's resource file*.

Statistics and probability

1.1 Introduction

How could a headteacher find out how many pupils in her school smoked regularly? What difficulties might be encountered in collecting the data?

The obvious way would be to ask them; perhaps in a school assembly or meeting she might ask smokers to raise their hands. As smoking is likely to be banned in school, she might find that very few smokers would give an honest response! It would certainly be necessary to hold a secret ballot of some sort, with each pupil, or a randomly selected sample of them, being sent a form to complete. Strict anonymity would have to be assured before she could anticipate a reliable result.

In your studies of statistics you should always be aware of the fact that your results and inferences are only as reliable as the means used to collect them. When you work on data which has been collected by other people, you should always consider **how** they collected it.

1

Reading suggestions

1	*Laws of the Game*	Eiger and Winkler	Penguin Books Ltd, 1983
2	*The Recursive Universe*	William Poundstone	Oxford University Press, 1985
3	*The Cosmic Blueprint*	Paul Davies	Heinemann, 1987
4	*God and the New Physics*	Paul Davies	Pelican, 1984
5	*The Blind Watchmaker*	Richard Dawkins	Longman, 1986
6	*The Selfish Gene*	Richard Dawkins	Paladin Books, 1979
7	*Chance and Necessity*	Jaques Monod	Fontana, 1974
8	*Order Out of Chaos*	Prigogine and Stengers	Fontana, 1985
9	*Invitation to Statistics*	Gavin Kennedy	Basil Blackwell Ltd, 1983
10	*The Mathematical Experience*	Davis and Hersh	Penguin Books Ltd, 1983
11	*Taking Risks*	Peter Sprent	Pelican, 1988
12	*Statistics in Action*	Peter Sprent	Pelican, 1977

1 and 2   illustrate general ideas of chance events in unusual and interesting situations.

5, 6 and 7   may be of greater interest to those studying biological sciences. 7 is a more difficult book.

3, 4 and 8   are concerned more with the physical sciences.

9 and 12   are general non-mathematical introductions to statistics – 9 has a strong historical perspective.

10   is a general mathematics reader, consisting of short articles on various themes. See for example 'The Coin of Tyche' for discussion of probability ideas.

11   considers real world encounters with risk and the analysis of uncertainty.

Regional trends

1 1976 – about 8%
1986 – about 21%

The figure is highest in the north of the UK, especially in Scotland and the North West. It is lowest in Northern Ireland.

2 (a) (i) 124.6
(ii) 69.5

(b) There are clear regional differences in GDP. The highest figures are found in London and the surrounding areas with a fall-off as you move north. Wales and Northern Ireland each have a low GDP in relation to the English regions and to Scotland.

3 (a) (i) About 22%   (ii) about 40%   (iii) about 38%

(b) No. Note also that the figures are for the 'clear up' of reported crime. Much crime is unreported and so cannot be 'cleared up'.

(c) (i) It takes time for a crime to be solved. You could find the percentage clear up rate by considering at some time the number of crimes reported – say, in a given month – and the number of these crimes solved after, say, six months. Once a suitable method is **defined**, each region must follow it carefully.

(ii) Data on **reported** crime could be collected easily from each region and suitably classified. It would be more difficult to obtain information on the hidden pool of unreported crime.

4 (a) Smoking in all regions shown has declined since 1976. There seems to be no obvious regional distinction.

(b) Directing advertising at suitable age groups might be sensible. You would need information on smoking habits, related to age groups and perhaps gender.

2 Exploratory data analysis

2.1 Introduction

> How might you decide if a Neighbourhood Watch Scheme in your area was successful? What data would you collect?

To decide if the Neighbourhood Watch Scheme was successful you would need to know something about previous crime statistics, perhaps focusing on particular crimes such as burglary, and how the data was collected. You would need to distinguish between crimes actually committed and those reported to the police. (There are likely to be fewer reported crimes.) Other conditions during the operation of the Neighbourhood Watch Scheme would need to remain the same to assess its value – for example, if police presence was drastically reduced this might affect the number of crimes committed.

You would need to define carefully **how** you would collect the data and what data you would collect.

2.2 Stem and leaf display

> Draw a stem and leaf diagram for the data for Bournemouth using intervals of 10°C, i.e. 10–19, 20–29.
> Also draw diagrams using intervals of 1°C and of 2°C.
> Which diagram do you think gives the best pictorial representation of the data?

Intervals of 10 °C

```
3 |
2 | 0 0 0 0 1 1 1 1 2 2 2 2 2 3 3 3 5 6 6 7
1 | 6 7 8 8 8 9                                   2|1 means 21 °C
0 |
```

Intervals of 1 °C

```
        ↑ etc.
  2 | 0000
  1 | 9
  1 | 888
  1 | 7
  1 | 6
  1 |
```

1|7 means 17 °C

Intervals of 2 °C

```
  2 | 6 6 7
  2 | 5
  2 | 2 2 2 2 2 3 3 3
  2 | 0 0 0 0 1 1 1 1
  1 | 8 8 8 9
  1 | 6 7
```

2|5 means 25 °C

The interval of 2 °C is probably the best. In the first plot, it is not possible to see any pattern – the grouping is too coarse. The plot using intervals of 1 °C also shows little pattern because it is very broken up.

2.3 Numerical representation of data

What properties do you think that a number should have if it is to be used to represent a set?

Describe situations where the most appropriate average would be

(a) the mode;

(b) the mean;

(c) the median.

Some desirable properties are:

- it should use all the data values;
- it should not be too influenced by 'wayward' values;
- it should be easy to calculate.

The **mode** is often used in situations where there are no numerical values, for example:

- the most common eye colour in a class;
- the university subject which attracts most students.

5

The ice dancers are concerned with their *total* score and so need a high **mean** mark. The mean is most frequently used in statistical work.

The **median** is usually very easy to calculate and is used for EDA work. It has the advantage that it tends to be little affected by a few abnormal items of data – it is more robust than the mean. In finding the median you **have** to use ranked data, that is data which are placed in order (for example the finishing position of a runner in her last 10 races, etc.)

2.4 Box and whisker diagrams

> Use the box plots shown above to compare and comment on the marking of the two examiners.
>
> Which examiner was the more lenient?
> Which was the more reliable?

A seems more reliable. Greater changes had to be made to the marking of B than of A. 50% of A's scripts needed at most a one mark change, while for B, 50% of scripts involved up to 3 marks in error.

B appears to have been more lenient than A. Most of B's scripts had marks taken off by the senior examiner.

The fact that the median lines are across the middles of the boxes indicates that the distributions are (roughly) symmetrical. However, the short whiskers on B's box plot indicate that his distribution is bimodal.

2.5 Constructing box plots

> Why would a stem plot be inappropriate for these data?

A stem plot shows every data point. With so much data and so many repeated values the stem plot would be very inconvenient. You are interested in questions such as, 'what percentage of patients stayed for longer than 10 days?' and you could not gain an impression of this **directly** from the stem plot.

Stem and leaf

1 By considering the data values alone it is difficult to say which of the two sets of heights is more variable. Certainly the male heights seem to be generally greater, but picking out which is the more variable is much harder.

2 (a)

	Husbands			Wives
18	0 2 4		18	
17	1 1 3 3 3 3 4 4 5 5 7 8		17	0 1
16	1 4 5 8		16	1 2 3 4
15			15	2 4 5 6 6 8 8 8 9 9 9
14			14	2
13			13	9

(b) There is an impression, from the diagrams, that the heights of the wives are more variable.

(c) The husbands have the higher middle value.

(d) Husbands: median = 173.5 cm.
Wives: median = 158 cm.

3

	Heights of 40 adult couples
18	0 2 4
17	0 1 1 1 3 3 3 3 4 4 5 5 7 8 9
16	1 1 2 3 4 4 5 8
15	2 4 5 6 6 8 8 8 9 9 9
14	2 3
13	9

The stem and leaf diagram has two peaks. The distribution is said to be bimodal (as opposed to the unimodal distributions of question 2(a)).

4 (d), as this reflects the indication of the stem and leaf plot. Such a distribution often occurs when two distinct populations are mixed.

Representative numbers for the average

1 Mean   = 4.4
Mode   = 5
Median = 5

Mean   This is the number of people per family if the 22 people are divided equally amongst the five families.
Mode   There are more families with 5 people than with any other number.
Median When the families are ranked in size, the middle family has 5 people.

2

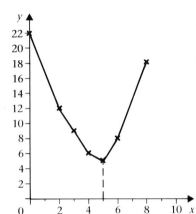

$y = |x - 2| + |x - 4| + |x - 5| + |x - 5| + |x - 6|$

Minimum at $x = 5$

Median = 5

3 (a) (i) Median = 3

   (ii)

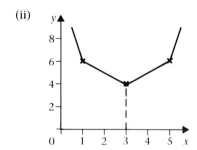

$y = |x - 1| + |x - 3| + |x - 5|$

Minimum $x = 3$

(b) In all cases, the total of the distances from x is least when x is equal to the median.

4 (a) (i)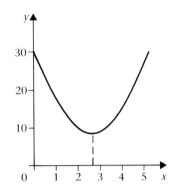

$$y = (x - 1)^2 + (x - 2)^2 + (x - 5)^2 = 3x^2 - 16x + 30$$

Minimum at $x = 2\frac{2}{3}$

(ii) This is the mean value of the data set 1, 2, 5.

(b) The sum of the squared distances from x is least when x is the mean value of the data set.

Cumulative frequency diagrams

1   The lower quartile is approximately 12.5 cm.
The upper quartile is approximately 18.5 cm.

2 (a)

Length (mm)	Cumulative frequency
Up to 110	4
Up to 125	14
Up to 140	33
Up to 155	69
Up to 170	112
Up to 185	138
Up to 200	147
Up to 215	150

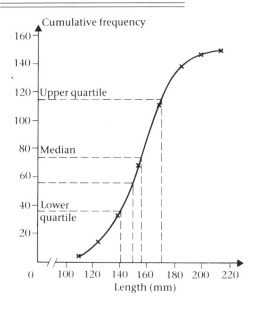

(b) The median is 156 mm.
The interquartile range is 30 mm.

(c) 56 worms are less than 150 mm
in length; that is 37%.

3 Data analysis revisited

3.1 Introduction

> Give some reasons why a census was thought to be important historically and why it is important today. To what uses can census data be put?

The most famous historical census is probably the *Domesday-book* which was commissioned by William the Conqueror to discover the value of his new kingdom. Census data was also used to aid tax collection and in preparation for war (see reference 9 in the reading list for a good historical perspective).

The modern census is wide-ranging and covers many aspects of our lives such as population patterns, mortality rates, number of home-owners, salary levels, and unemployment statistics. Information is normally presented on a regional and national basis.

The data can be used in various ways. Examples might be: planning for demographic changes or deciding on transport development for a particular region. It can also be used to examine national or local trends and to answer questions such as: 'How many mothers work outside the home?' 'Are people getting married later in life?' etc.

3.3 Representing grouped data – histograms

> Draw a frequency diagram for the data as presented. Re-group the data into the intervals: 5–15, 15–17.5, 17.5–20, 20–22.5, 22.5–30 and redraw the diagram.
>
> Comment on whether this sort of diagram provides a good representation of the data.

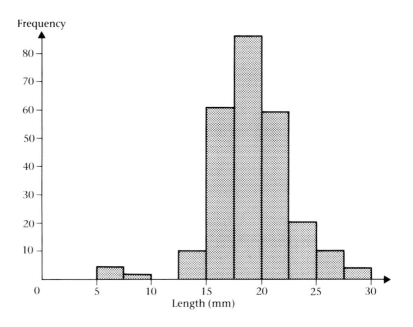

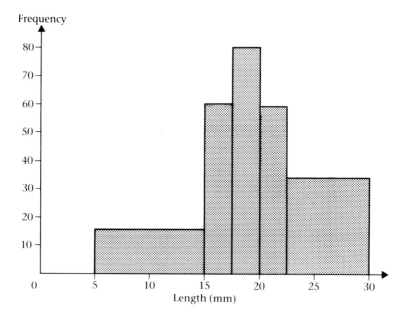

The second bar-chart is not a fair representation of the data. For example, from the diagram it looks as though there are only just over twice as many rods in the 17.5–20 mm range as in each of the ranges 22.5–25 mm, 25–27.5 mm and 27.5–30 mm. In fact there are twice as many rods in the 17.5–20 mm range as in all the last three intervals combined. The diagram has not taken into account the fact that the intervals are of **different** widths.

3.5 Averages and spread

> What might be a sensible reference point? Define a measure of spread about this point.

The obvious points about which to measure spread would seem to be the median and the mean, as they represent 'average' values for the data.

You have already met one measure of spread which is measured about the median – the interquartile range. It has the disadvantage of being insensitive to changes in the 'outer' 50% of the data. A possible measure of spread around the mean is:

the sum of the differences from the mean, i.e. $\sum(x - \bar{x})$.

With this, however, negative differences cancel each other out and the result is **always** zero. This problem with negative differences can be solved in two ways, by considering either

the sum of the squares of the differences $\qquad \sum(x - \bar{x})^2;$

or the sum of the absolute value of the $\qquad \sum|x - \bar{x}|.$
differences

A measure of spread should not be dependent on the number of values in the sample, so an 'average' needs to be taken. It should be in the same units as the original data – if the observations are measured in centimetres then the measure of spread should also be in centimetres.

3.7 Variance for frequency distributions

Show that for a frequency distribution

$$x = \frac{\sum xf}{\sum f}, \text{ variance} = \frac{\sum (x - \bar{x})^2 f}{\sum f}$$

In the general case:

data values	Frequency of data values	group total of data values	group total of squared deviation from $\bar{x}$
x_1	f_1	$x_1 \times f_1$	$(x_1 - \bar{x})^2 \times f_1$
x_2	f_2	$x_2 \times f_2$	$(x_2 - \bar{x})^2 \times f_2$
x_3	f_3	$x_3 \times f_3$	$(x_3 - \bar{x})^2 \times f_3$
•	•	•	•
•	•	•	•
•	•	•	•
x_n	f_n	$x_n \times f_n$	$(x_n - \bar{x})^2 \times f_n$
Total	$n = \sum f$	$\sum xf$	$\sum (x - \bar{x})^2 f$

$$\text{mean; } \bar{x} \; \frac{\sum xf}{\sum f} \qquad \text{variance; } \frac{\sum (x - \bar{x}(^2 f}{\sum f}$$

Standard deviation and variance

1 Mean, $\bar{x} = \dfrac{5.7 + 5.8 + 5.7 + 5.8 + 5.8 + 5.8}{6}$

$\qquad\qquad = 5.77$ (to 3 s.f.)

$\sum(x - \bar{x})^2 = (5.7 - 5.77)^2 + (5.8 - 5.77)^2 + (5.7 - 5.77)^2 + (5.8 - 5.77)^2$
$\qquad\qquad + (5.8 - 5.77)^2 + (5.8 - 5.77)^2$
$\qquad\qquad = 0.013$ (to 2 s.f.)

2 The variance 0.0022 for couple A $= \dfrac{0.013}{6}$ to 2 s.f.)

$\quad$ The variance for couple B $= \dfrac{0.953}{6} = 0.16$ (to 2 s.f.)

3 The standard deviation of couple A's scores is $\sqrt{0.0022} = 0.047$ (to 2 s.f.).

$\quad$ The standard deviation of couple B's scores is $\sqrt{0.016} = 0.40$ (to 2 s.f.).

4 (a) 0. The points are all the same and have no spread. This is shown by a standard deviation of zero.

$\quad$ (b) 1.4 (to 2 s.f.)

$\quad$ (c) 1.7 (to 2 s.f.). Set (c) is slightly more spread out than (b) and has a correspondingly higher standard deviation.

$\quad$ (d) 2.8 (to 2 s.f.). Set (d) is twice as spread out as set (b) and has twice the standard deviation.

5 (a) If all the values are increased by the same number, then the mean is also increased by this number but the standard deviation is unchanged.

$\quad$ (b) If all the values are multiplied by the same number, then the mean and the standard deviation are also multiplied by that number.

Variance by direct calculation

1 (a) 2.125

   (b) 68.$\dot{2}$.

   The calculation of $(x - \bar{x})^2$ for all values of x would prove to be cumbersome for large data values, making the algorithm very labour intensive! Also, it requires two 'runs' through the data.

2 $\dfrac{a^2 + b^2 + c^2}{3} - \bar{x}^2$

3 (a) $\dfrac{a^2 + b^2 + c^2 + d^2}{4} - \bar{x}^2$

   (b) $\dfrac{\sum x^2}{n} - \bar{x}^2$

4 (a) 2.125

   (b) 68.$\dot{2}$

   The second algorithm requires fewer calculations and only one run through the data.

5

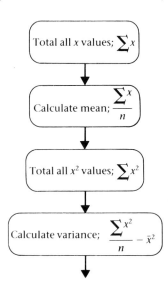

4 Probability models 1

4.1 Introduction

(a) Does the evidence in the cartoon prove Murphy's law?

(b) Would Murphy's law be proved if 70 out of 100 pieces landed butter-side down?

(c) Use the random number generating function on a computer or programmable calculator to simulate the situation described in the illustration. Help is given on technology datasheet: *Toast*.

(a, b) Statistical data can never prove a theory; it can only indicate its likelihood or otherwise. If you tossed a coin ten times and obtained seven heads, then this would not be 'out of the ordinary' and would certainly not imply that the coin was biased. Even ten heads from ten throws occurs occasionally with a fair coin. However, large amounts of data can make certain conclusions more likely than others. For instance, obtaining over 70 heads out of 100 with an unbiased coin is very unlikely, and so would provide strong evidence of bias; over 700 out of 1000 would provide even stronger evidence.

It is the accumulation of statistical evidence which supports belief in certain theories. For example, there were initially no scientific reasons to suggest that smoking caused lung cancer. It was only when large amounts of statistical evidence were collected which compared the incidence of cancer in smokers and non-smokers that the connection was made. This in itself does not prove a causal connection; it simply makes the lack of such a connection extremely unlikely.

In the cartoon, **neither** statement is correct. You can never 'prove' how lucky or unlucky you are, but you can investigate the chances of certain things happening. In games such as poker, the concept of 'luck' is less important than the ability to weigh up the chances of certain events occurring. For this reason, gambling played an important role in motivating the initial development of probability theory.

(c)   You should find that 7 or more slices butter-side down occurs about one time in five, which is quite often.

The probability of getting over 70 out of 100 butter-downs is about 3×10^{-5}! So if this actually happened, it would certainly support Murphy's law. But it would not **prove** it, since there is a non-zero probability of the result occurring assuming Murphy's law were false. In the language of statistics, the results would be highly **significant.** These ideas are explored further in chapter 6.

4.3   Random variables: discrete or continuous?

> Which of the variables above are:
>
> (a) continuous;   (b) discrete?

C, S, T are certainly discrete. H and W are continuous. G, the proportion of children in a family that are girls, is discrete, taking only the possible values $\frac{0}{n}, \frac{1}{n}, \frac{2}{n}$, etc., where n is the number of children in the family.

A, the age of a child, is normally given in whole (completed) years (for example 12 years old, etc.). The 'real' age is a continuous variable.

Other examples of discrete random variables are:

number of eggs in a clutch;
number of coin tosses needed to obtain a head;
number of people in a queue;
number of rainy days in a month.

A continuous random variable is any continuous quantity (weight, height, length, time, distance, area, volume, etc.) subject to random variation, for instance:

the duration of a television programme selected at random;
the wingspan of a seagull;
the weight of a bag of potatoes.

Notice that any measurement of a continuous variable is of necessity discrete, since any measuring instrument can only work to a certain accuracy (for example to the nearest mm, millisecond, etc.).

In statistics, a distinction is made between discrete and continuous probability models.

Chance cards 1

1   Even though the result of each cut is random (provided you shuffle and cut so that each card has an equal chance of selection) the cumulative results so far give you some idea of the composition of the packs. For example, you may have found that there seem to be more 1s and 4s, but this could be a chance result. You would need to cut your pack a much larger number of times to become more certain, or to make a more detailed hypothesis about the composition of the pack.

2   (a, b) By the time you have simulated 1000 cuts of your pack, you should expect the relative frequencies to be pretty close to the probabilities of cutting a 1, 2, 3 and 4. They are still only approximate and if you were to run the program again you would get different values for the relative frequencies. However, **in the long run** you would expect these to stabilise and tend to the probabilities, which are fixed, but often unknown.

    (c)   In this case, you can actually calculate the values of the probabilities by inspecting the packs, assuming that in a random cut of the pack each card has an equal likelihood of being selected. The composition of the yellow pack and the probability distributions are as follows:

Yellow pack

	1	2	3	4
No. in pack	16	12	8	4
Probability	0.4	0.3	0.2	0.1

The shape of the distributions you have drawn for 50, 100, 500 and 1000 trials approaches this probability distribution as the number of trials increases.

3   The probability distributions for the red and the blue packs are as follows:

Red pack

	1	2	3	4
No. in pack	10	10	10	10
Probability	0.25	0.25	0.25	0.25

Blue pack

	1	2	3	4
No. in pack	10	20	10	0
Probability	0.25	0.5	0.25	0

4 The probability distribution from a large number of trials appears to be as follows:

g	1	2	3	4
$P(G = g)$	1	0	0	0

so the composition of the pack would seem to be forty 1s and no 2s, 3s or 4s. However, you can never be certain of this.

The only certain deduction you can make is that there is at least one card numbered '1'!

Chance cards 2

1   Just as the relative frequency of each result stabilises as the number of cuts increases, the mean winnings per game also 'evens out'. So your value for 10000 games should be the best answer here. If you repeat the simulation again using $n = 10000$, you should obtain a similar value for the sample mean.

   £2 would be a reasonable charge for the bank to break even. Of course, in real games, the stake is fixed so that on average the bank makes a profit!

2   Total winnings = £$(1 \times 400 + 2 \times 300 + 3 \times 200 + 4 \times 100)$
                    = £2000

   So mean winnings = £$\dfrac{2000}{1000}$
                    = £2 per game

3   (a)   Mean $\mu = 1 \times 0.25 + 2 \times 0.25 + 3 \times 0.25 + 4 \times 0.25$
              = 2.5

   (b)   You should notice that as n increases you get closer to the mean of the probability distribution.

4   (a)   Mean $\mu = 1 \times 0.25 + 2 \times 0.5 + 3 \times 0.25 + 4 \times 0 = 2$

   (b)   You should find that the sample means for B get closer to 2 (the mean of the probability distribution) as n gets larger and larger.

The nuclear reactor

1   The more free neutrons are provided initially, the less likely it is that all are absorbed, and so the more likely it is that the reaction will continue.

2   When $p = 0.4$, the reaction always dies; with $p = 0.6$, the reaction grows rapidly, unless you start with a small number of free neutrons, and they are all absorbed. This is unlikely, but not impossible!

When $p = 0.5$, as predicted in 1, the reaction is stable provided sufficient free neutrons are provided initially to make total absorption unlikely.

3   The probability distribution for the random variable X is:

x	0	2
$P(X = x)$	$1 - p$	p

where p = probability of collision

So $\mu = 0 \times (1 - p) + 2 \times p = 2p$.

If $p > 0.5$, then $\mu > 1$, and the reaction expands.

If $p < 0.5$, then $\mu < 1$, and the reaction dies.

If $p = 0.5$, then $\mu = 1$, and the reaction is stable.

4   The probability distribution is now:

x	0	1	2
$P(X = x)$	$1 - p$	$\frac{1}{2}p$	$\frac{1}{2}p$

So $\mu = 0 \times (1 - p) + 1 \times \frac{1}{2}p + 2 \times \frac{1}{2}p = \frac{3}{2}p$

The value of p which produces a stable reaction is $\frac{2}{3}$.

Notice how the apparently random behaviour of the individual free neutrons produces a pattern which can be predicted from the probability model – order out of chaos.

5   Here are three suggested limitations of the model:

(a) The probability of collision and absorption will not remain constant. They depend on the density of the free neutrons in each part of the reactor, which is not constant.

(b) The reaction does not take place in 'rounds': free neutrons are being produced and absorbed continuously.

(c) While most of the free neutrons are absorbed using graphite rods, there is also a probability of leakage through the shielding surrounding the reactor. Free neutrons with paths close to the boundary are more likely to leak in this way.

The fly

1 Starting with 10 females, the population will usually survive and increase – but not always.

2 With larger initial populations, the chances of extinction become less, and the population usually reaches plague proportions. However, regardless of the initial population, there is always a non-zero probability of extinction.

3 $\mu = 0 \times \frac{1}{3} + 1 \times \frac{1}{3} + 2 \times \frac{1}{6} + 3 \times \frac{1}{6} = 1\frac{1}{6}$

So on average each female produces $1\frac{1}{6}$ females for the next generation, and the population usually grows.

4 (i) 0.9   (ii) 1.1   (iii) 1   (iv) 1

Although (iii) and (iv) both have mean 1 and so should produce stable populations, (iv) is more vulnerable since it has a higher variance. This means the population fluctuates more dramatically and is more likely to become zero by chance.

6 Here are three suggested limitations:

(a) The population of males is ignored. It takes two to reproduce!

(b) Lifetimes vary, and so generations cannot be counted on a weekly basis.

(c) In practice, populations are controlled by predators and by availability of food.

Populations are not usually modelled mathematically by a 'discrete' model such as this, but by a continuous model where the population numbers are regarded as being continuous variables in time whose values are modelled by 'differential equations'. However, discrete models are still valuable in some cases.

5 Probability models 2

5.1 Multiplying probabilities

> Suppose that the darts player above hits treble 20 with one dart in five on average.
>
> What is the probability of her scoring 180 with three darts?
>
> Comment on any assumptions you have made.

The answer $\frac{1}{125}$ can be seen in many ways. For example, imagine that the darts player has a large number of attempts at throwing three darts.

She would expect to score triple twenty with the first dart on $\frac{1}{5}$ of the occasions.

On $\frac{1}{5}$ of this reduced number of occasions she would also expect to score triple twenty with the second dart.

The number of times a triple twenty would be scored on all three throws is $\frac{1}{5} \times \frac{1}{5} \times \frac{1}{5}$ of the total number of attempts.

In practice, it is likely that scoring triple twenties with the first two darts will affect the chance of scoring triple twenty with the third dart. The chances may be increased if the darts player scores two triple twenties because she is on good form. Alternatively, the chances may be reduced if the first two darts block the triple twenty.

5.2 Adding probabilities

Discuss whether the following pairs of events are mutually exclusive and whether they are independent.

(a) The weather is fine; I walk to work.

(b) I cut an ace; you cut a king.

(c) Dan's Delight wins next Saturday's 2:30 race at Newbury; Andy's Nag wins next Saturday's 2:30 race at Newbury.

(d) Dan's Delight wins next Saturday's 2:30 race at Newbury; Andy's Nag wins next Saturday's 3:15 race at Newbury.

(e) Mrs Smith has toothache today; Mr Smith has toothache today.

(f) Mrs Smith has a cold today; Mr Smith has a cold today.

(a) The two events are probably dependent, i.e. I am more likely to walk to work if the weather is fine. They are very unlikely to be mutually exclusive!

(b) My cutting an ace and your cutting a king are independent events if the ace is replaced in the pack. They are **not** mutually exclusive.

(c) If Dan's Delight wins, Andy's Nag cannot – the events are mutually exclusive. They must therefore be dependent as the occurrence of one obviously affects the other.

(d) There is no relationship. The events are independent. They are **not** mutually exclusive.

(e) Since Mrs Smith having toothache is not likely to influence whether Mr Smith has one also, the events are likely to be independent. They are not mutually exclusive.

(f) There is likely to be some connection here and the events are probably not independent, nor are they mutually exclusive.

5.4 The binostat

> The picture shows that more balls collect in the central slots than in the outside slots. Why do you think this happens?

There are more paths leading to a central slot than to an outside one. Assuming that each path is equally likely to be taken by a ball, more balls will end up in the central slots than in the outside ones.

5.5 Unequal probabilities

> What assumptions are being made in this binomial model?
>
> How valid do you think these are?

(a) The seeds must be of uniform quality so that the probability of **each** seed germinating is 0.9.

(b) The probability of germination must be independent of both the soil conditions at the planting site and the weather after planting.

Neither of these assumptions will be precisely true. However, in practice, the binomial model will be a reasonable approximation unless the assumptions are grossly contravened, for example by planting the seeds just before a heavy frost.

5.6 Making inferences

> In making a test of this kind, explain why it is sensible to consider a result of **seven or more** slices landing 'butter down'.

No matter what the probability is for a single slice landing 'butter-side down', getting **exactly** seven slices out of ten 'butter down' will have a fairly low probability, and so considering the probability of this event does not help to decide about Murphy's law.

The probability of an event such as 'seven or more butter-side down' is a much more discriminating test of the proposed model.

Snap

1 $40 \times 40 = 1600$ possible pairs

2 (a) $16 \times 10 = 160$ possible double ones

  (b) $12 \times 10 = 120$ double twos

  (c) $8 \times 10 = 80$ double threes

  (d) $4 \times 10 = 40$ double fours

  (e) $160 + 120 + 80 + 40 = 400$

3 (a) P(double one) $= \frac{160}{1600} = \frac{1}{10} = 0.1$

  (b) $\frac{120}{1600} = \frac{3}{40} = 0.075$

  (c) $\frac{400}{1600} = \frac{1}{4} = 0.25$

4 The probability of, say, double two is: P(Yellow 2 **and** Red 2) $=$ P(Y2) $\times$ P(R2)
$$= 0.3 \times 0.25$$
$$= 0.075$$

The probability of a double is as follows:

P(double one **or** double two **or** . . .) $=$ P(double one) $+$ P(double two) $+$ . . .
$$= \text{P(Y1 and R1)} + \text{P(Y2 and R2)} + \ldots$$
$$= 0.4 \times 0.25 + 0.3 \times 0.25 + 0.2 \times 0.25$$
$$+ 0.1 \times 0.25$$
P(double one **or** double two **or** . . .) $= 0.25$

5 Snap occurs when you obtain:

(B1 **and** Y1) or (B2 **and** Y2) or (B3 **and** Y3)

So P(Snap) $= (\frac{1}{4} \times \frac{4}{10}) + (\frac{1}{2} \times \frac{3}{10}) + (\frac{1}{4} \times \frac{2}{10}) = \frac{12}{40} = 0.3$

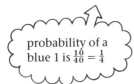

probability of a blue 1 is $\frac{10}{40} = \frac{1}{4}$

The binostat

1 There are three routes; each one is equally likely and each has probability $\frac{1}{8}$. Therefore P (slot 1) = $\frac{3}{8}$.

2

x	0	1	2	3
$P(X = x)$	$\frac{1}{8}$	$\frac{3}{8}$	$\frac{3}{8}$	$\frac{1}{8}$

3 For 400 balls you would expect $400 \times \frac{1}{8} = 50$ in slot 0, etc.

Slot X	0	1	2	3
Expected number	50	150	150	50

The 'Bino' simulation should reproduce these results approximately – the **probabilities** from your run of 'Bino' should be near $\frac{1}{8}, \frac{3}{8}, \frac{3}{8}$ and $\frac{1}{8}$.

4

x	0	1	2
$P(X = x)$	$\frac{1}{4}$	$\frac{1}{2}$	$\frac{1}{4}$

Expected frequencies are 100, 200, 100.

5 The ball will hit 4 pins. The probability of a particular route is $(\frac{1}{2})^4 = \frac{1}{16}$.

6 Routes to $P = 1$. Routes to $Q = 3$.

There are therefore $1 + 3 = 4$ routes to slot 1. P(slot 1) = $\frac{4}{16} = \frac{1}{4}$.

7

Slot x	0	1	2	3	4
Routes	1	4	6	4	1

x	0	1	2	3	4
$P(x)$	$\frac{1}{16}$	$\frac{4}{16}$	$\frac{6}{16}$	$\frac{4}{16}$	$\frac{1}{16}$

8 You would expect the number of balls in the slots to be 50, 200, 300, 200, 50.

The biased binostat

1 The ball is deflected R L R. The probability that the ball will take the route shown is $0.4 \times 0.6 \times 0.4 = 0.096$.

Assume that each deflection (L or R) is independent of previous ones.

2 Other routes are R R L and L R R. The probabilities are both $0.4^2 \times 0.6 = 0.096$.

3 P(slot 2) = $3 \times 0.096 = 0.288$

There are 3 equally likely ways to arrive in slot 2.

4 $\begin{aligned} &\text{P(slot 0)} = 1 \times (0.6)^3 &&= 0.216 \quad \text{Route: L L L} \\ &\text{P(slot 1)} = 3 \times (0.6)^2 (0.4) = 0.432 \quad \text{Routes: L L R, L R L, R L L} \\ &\text{P(slot 3)} = 1 \times (0.4)^3 &&= 0.064 \quad \text{Route: R R R} \end{aligned}$

5 The expected frequencies are

Slot	0	1	2	3
Number of balls	108	216	144	32

6

x	$P(X = x)$		
0	$1 \times (0.6)^5$	$=$	0.07776
1	$5 \times (0.4) \times (0.6)^4$	$=$	0.2592
2	$10 \times (0.4)^2 \times (0.6)^3$	$=$	0.3456
3	$10 \times (0.4)^3 \times (0.6)^2$	$=$	0.2304
4	$5 \times (0.4)^4 \times (0.6)$	$=$	0.0768
5	$1 \times (0.4)^5$	$=$	0.01024

7

x	$P(X = x)$		
0	$1 \times (0.2)^3$	$=$	0.008
1	$3 \times (0.8) \times (0.2)^2$	$=$	0.096
2	$3 \times (0.8)^2 \times (0.2)$	$=$	0.384
3	$1 \times (0.8)^3$	$=$	0.512

6 Sampling

6.1 Introduction

> By considering the illustrations above and some examples of your own, think of various different reasons why you might want to use a sample rather than test every member of the population.
>
> What makes for a 'good' sample?

There are several reasons why you might wish to sample a parent population rather than test every member of the population.

(a) There would be little point in a car manufacturer testing every car produced in this fashion. There would be no cars left to sell! Some items need to be 'tested to destruction' to see how strong or safe they are. Motorcycle helmets, climbers' ropes and steel for building bridges are some examples.

(b) If you wanted people's opinions about something, for example which party they would vote for if there were a general election tomorrow, it would be very costly and time-consuming to interview every voter in the country.

When you next read about a survey in a newspaper look to see what size of sample the results are based on.

(c) Wine tasters sample just a small mouthful of wine to judge its quality. Sampling from a large vat of wine enables the quality of hundreds of bottles to be ascertained.

A 'good' sample should

(i) be representative of the parent population;

(ii) enable you to find out what you want to know about the parent population.

6.5 **Further Testing**

> What would the manufacturer of Wolfit like you to infer from this claim?
>
> Does the survey of dogs support the intended inference?

They would hope that you might infer that 80% of dogs prefer Wolfit.

The evidence here is based on a single sample of 10 dogs – it may not even be a representative sample of all dogs. Even if only 50% of dogs prefer Wolfit, there is a chance that as many as 8 out of 10 would choose it in a random trial. In this section you will study whether the result of this trial does at least indicate that there is some preference for Wolfit amongst dogs.

Bias

> For a small class it may be necessary for each pupil to take two or more samples using each window.

It is quite likely that neither 'window' gives particularly close estimates to the true mean (μ). Neither sampling method is likely to give a representative sample, due in part to the way in which the data is listed on the sheet. Window A will always give a sample of five students of the same sex, while window B will sometimes give a mixed group. Neither will give a sample of five independently selected individuals. If a particular sixth former is selected, then the other members of the sample are adjacent or close by on the list.

To obtain a more representative sample, you must ensure that each member of the population has an equal and independent chance of being included. This type of sample is called a **random sample.** An elementary but time-consuming way of obtaining such a sample would be to number the sixth formers from 1 to 300 and then to draw five numbers from 300 well-mixed raffle tickets.

A microcomputer or calculator can be used to rapidly generate random numbers in the range 1 to 300. Some calculators generate random integers in the range 0 to 9, so three such numbers taken together give a number in the range 000 to 999, each with an equal probability of occurring. If each sixth former is allocated one number you would not be able to make a selection if any of random numbers 301–999 appeared. To avoid this wastage you can allocate three numbers to each person.

	Numbers allocated		
Student 1	001	301	601
Student 2	002	302	602
. . . .	. . .	. . .	. . .
. . . .	. . .	. . .	. . .
Student 300	300	600	900

In this scheme only the numbers 000 and 901–999 remain unused. However, it is not possible to allocate these numbers, as each sixth former must have an equal number of 'chances' so that each has an equal probability of $\frac{1}{300}$ of being included in the sample.

Sample size

1   Starting at the same place in the table would produce identical samples! Each student should therefore use a different part of the table.

2   You should find that the distribution of $\bar{x}$ for random samples of size 10 is a more compact and symmetrical distribution than that for $\bar{x}$ from random samples of 5. Your results should be close to these:

Size of random sample	Mean of $\bar{x}$	Variance of $\bar{x}$
5	167.4	8.63
10	167.4	4.31

The distribution obtained using the windows is less likely to be close to these results.

3   **Typical results for sample means**

100 samples $n = 5$		100 samples $n = 10$	
$\bar{x}$	f	$\bar{x}$	f
157–	0	157–	0
159–	3	159–	0
161–	6	161–	4
163–	18	163–	15
165–	21	165–	28
167–	26	167–	32
169–	13	169–	17
171–	8	171–	3
173–	5	173–	1
175–	0	175–	0
177–	0	177–	0

mean of $\bar{x}$: 167.1   variance of $\bar{x}$: 10.7   mean of $\bar{x}$: 167.2   variance of $\bar{x}$: 5.2

4   Results for both samples of size 5 and size 10 are likely to be close to the true mean.

5   A crucial part of the theory underpinning the use of samples is that as the sample size increases, the distribution of the sample mean becomes increasingly clustered around the true value of the population mean. This is reflected in the smaller variance of the distribution of $\bar{x}$ for samples of size 10 as compared to samples of size 5. The estimates generated by larger random samples are less variable than those generated by smaller random samples so, as you might expect, unusual results from large samples tend to be more **significant** than those from small samples.

Simulations

1 Since no samples in the simulation produced a result as low as five supporting the scheme, it seems highly likely that the actual percentage in support is less than 50%.

2 (b) The results of a simulation depend upon chance factors and so each time a simulation is run you would expect the results to be slightly different.

3 A result of 22 is in or near the middle of the distribution – it is the sort of result you would expect if the initial assumption was valid. It would then be quite likely that around 50% of the population were in favour of the monorail.

4 About 10% of the samples will have 25 or more teenagers drinking the brand.

   You cannot be reasonably sure that the campaign has been a success.

5 (a) For a large number of samples, the coin should come down heads three times or less for about 17% of the time.

   There is some suspicion of bias but such a result is to be expected about one time out of six.

   (b) The chance of a coin coming down heads thirty times or less out of one hundred tosses is less than 0.01%.

   It is therefore reasonable to suspect that the coin is biased.

6 For an unbiased die you would expect to get eight or fewer sixes about 3% of the time.

   There is a suspicion of bias.